cloverleaf books™

Planet Protectors

Watch Over Our Water

Lisa Bullard

illustrated by **Xiao Xin**

M MILLBROOK PRESS · MINNEAPOLIS

For Dad—L.B.

Millbrook Press
A division of Lerner Publishing Group, Inc.
241 First Avenue North
Minneapolis, MN 55401 U.S.A.

Website address: www.lernerbooks.com

Main body text set in Slappy Inline 18/28. Typeface provided by T26.

Library of Congress Cataloging-in-Publication Data

Bullard, Lisa.
    Watch over our water / by Lisa Bullard ; illustrated by Xiao Xin.
        p.   cm. — (Cloverleaf books—planet protectors)
    Includes index.
    ISBN 978-0-7613-6106-0 (lib. bdg. : alk. paper)
    1. Water—Juvenile literature. 2. Water—Pollution—Juvenile literature.
I. Xin, Xiao, ill. II. Title.
GB662.3.B85 2012
333.91'16—dc22   2010053299

Manufactured in the United States of America
1 – BP – 7/15/11

TABLE OF CONTENTS

Chapter One
More Important Than Root Beer.....4

Chapter Two
Stop Water Waste.....10

Chapter Three
Keep Water Clean.....16

Stop the Sneaky Leaks....22

Glossary....23

To Learn More....24

Index....24

More Important Than Root Beer

Hi! I'm Trina. I'm working to be an **Earth saver**. So today, I made an Earth map.

The Earth has so much **water**,
I almost ran out of blue marker!

I guess I'd better think about water
if I'm going to save the Earth.

Dad agrees water is really important.
He says that more than half of a
human body is **made of water.**

Do you think that means we have

fish swimming around inside?

Plants, animals, and people need water to live. And people use water for more than just **drinking**.

We use it to **grow food**.

We use it to get **clean**.

If you think about it, water's even more important than root beer.

Chapter Two

Stop Water Waste

Almost all of the **Earth's water** is salty ocean water. Yuck! Drinking too much of it makes us sick.

Some of the water we drink comes from underground. Other drinking water comes from lakes, streams, and rivers. This water is not salty like ocean water.

The Earth doesn't really have a lot of drinkable water. So we **can't waste** it.

My teacher says even kids can **conserve water**. *Conserve* means "to not waste it." She says taking a fast shower uses less water than taking a bath.

There are lots of ways to conserve water. Turn off the water while you brush your teeth. Keep drinking water in the refrigerator. Then you don't have to run the faucet until it's cold. Do you wait until the shower water is hot before getting in? Catch the water in a pail while you wait. Use it to water plants or wash your dog.

But I have a better idea. I'll just stay dirty!

Lots of wasted water goes down the toilet. So my family has a special rule when we're at home.

We say, "If it's pee, let it be."

People have gotten smarter about how to make toilets. The new ones use lots less water than old toilets. Maybe your family could save money for a new toilet? There are other ways to use less water in your toilet too. Ask a grown-up to look online.

Don't think of it as gross. It's saving Earth's water, one less flush at a time.

Chapter Three
Keep Water Clean

My dog, Daisy, creates another problem. Her toilet is outside. I don't want her dog doo washing into the water underground. So I clean up after Daisy.

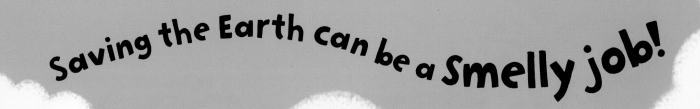

Saving the Earth can be a **Smelly job!**

You can buy special trash bags for pet cleanup. They break down more quickly than other bags. That means they are better for the Earth.

Litter often gets washed into lakes and rivers. This also makes the water dirty.

Make sure you put your trash where it belongs.
Otherwise, I might end up drinking it.

Dirty water can make people sick. It is also bad for fish, animals, and plants. They can die if their water becomes too dirty.

Maybe you could help me conserve water?

And keep it clean?

20

Then I can find another way to save the Earth tomorrow.

Stop the Sneaky Leaks

Does your family have a sneaky leak? Sometimes the problem is a drippy faucet. Go around your home and do a "leak peek." Listen for a drip, drip, drip sound at each faucet. Little drips add up to a big waste of water.

It's easy to test your toilets for leaks too. Ask a grown-up to lift the top off the toilet tank. The tank is the part behind the toilet seat. It holds water for the next flush. Put a few drops of food color in the tank. Put the top back on. Don't flush the toilet yet!

Now you have to wait. Thirty minutes is long enough. Go back and look in the toilet bowl (not the tank). Has the water changed color? If the answer is yes, you have a sneaky leak.

Let a grown-up know if you find any leaks. Fixing leaks means less wasted water. It also saves your family money. Maybe you can buy something tasty with the savings. One root beer float coming up!

GLOSSARY

conserve: to keep something from being wasted

drinkable: safe to drink

flush: to clean something out with a large amount of water

leak: a hole or break that lets water escape

litter: trash that people leave lying around

BOOKS

Green, Jen. *Why Should I Save Water?* Hauppauge, NY: Barron's Educational Series, 2005.
This book will give you more ideas for ways you can save water.

Hock, Peggy. *Our Earth: Saving Water.* New York, Children's Press, 2009. This book talks about where water comes from. It also talks about how to make sure we have enough clean water.

Nelson, Robin. *We Use Water.* Minneapolis: Lerner Publications Company, 2003.
Bright photos in this book show some of the many ways we use water.

WEBSITES

Canadian Waters: The Big Blue Bus Kid's Corner
http://www.dfo-mpo.gc.ca/canwaters-eauxcan/bbb-lgb/index_e.asp
This website is from the government of Canada. The site has lots of water activities and fun things to learn.

EPA: Water
http://www.epa.gov/kids/water.htm
This website from the Environmental Protection Agency has games and activities.
They will help you learn about the water cycle and more.

PBS KIDS GO!: EekoWorld
http://pbskids.org/eekoworld/index.html?load=air_water
Visit this website from PBS Kids to see a movie about water.

conserve water, 12—13, 20

dirty water, 18—19

drinking water, 10—11

leaks, 22

litter, 18

ocean water, 10

toilets, 14—16, 22

water underground, 10, 16

ways we use water, 8—9